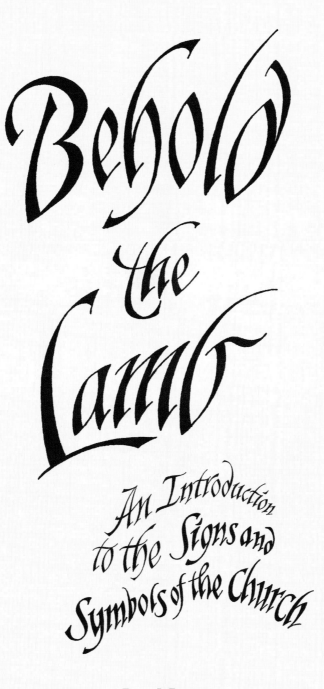

Behold the Lamb

An Introduction to the Signs and Symbols of the Church

PAMELA J. NIELSEN

ILLUSTRATED BY ARTHUR KIRCHHOFF

CALLIGRAPHY BY EDWARD Q. LUHMANN

CONCORDIA PUBLISHING HOUSE • SAINT LOUIS

1   2   3   4   5   6   7   8   9   10   18   17   16   15   14   13   12   11   10   09

On my heart imprint Your image,
Blessed Jesus, King of grace,
That life's riches, cares, and pleasures
Never may Your work erase;
Let the clear inscription be: Jesus, crucified for me,
Is my life, my hope's foundation,
And my glory and salvation! *LSB 422*

*For **Kristin**, dear goddaughter and niece.*

*With gratitude for my parents, and the teachers, pastors,
and professors whom God has used to imprint His image in my life.
Through their faithful proclamation and teaching of
the story, language, symbols, music, culture, and rituals of
the Christian faith I became acquainted with a flesh
and blood Savior who entered this world to rescue me
from the very real perils of sin, death, and the devil.*

What are Symbols?

The next day he saw Jesus coming toward him, and said,
"Behold, the Lamb of God, who takes away the sin of the world!"

JOHN 1:29

God gave John the Baptist eyes of faith to see that Jesus truly is the Lamb of God who came into this world to save all people.

When sin entered the world through Adam and Eve, our heavenly Father promised to provide forgiveness and salvation through a Messiah, a savior from sin. This Savior would become the ultimate and perfect **sacrifice** for sin. As God's people waited and watched for the promised sacrifice, they offered lamb and other animals on **altars** as payment for their sins. The value of these sacrifices was that they pointed God's Son, Jesus Christ, as the only sacrifice that would destroy sin. Jesus' suffering, death, and resurrection is the sacrifice that won victory over sin and death for all people.

John the Baptist's words tell a story and give us images that help us understand what he is saying. From the beginning, God has used language, which forms pictures in our minds when He talks to us. The Christian Church, too, has used the language of pictures or **symbols** to point people to God, who is our only salvation from sin, death, and the devil.

4

Today, when God's people see an image of a lamb with a victory flag, they understand that this is a symbol of Jesus, who died on the cross to take away the sin of the world.

You may already know many of the symbols used to tell the Church's story of salvation because they are found many places in your church, such as on the walls, windows, banners, and altar. No matter which symbol you look at, all are part of the story of your salvation, each symbol pointing you to the Lamb of God who takes away the sin of the world!

Symbols about God

Now when all the people were baptized, and when Jesus
also had been baptized and was praying, the heavens were opened, and
the Holy Spirit descended on Him in bodily form, like a dove;
and a voice came from heaven, "You are My beloved Son;
with You I am well pleased."

LUKE 3:21–22

Our God, the only true God, is a **triune** God. Triune means "three
in one." The true God is three distinct persons in one divine being.
How this is possible is a mystery that we cannot explain or understand.

The Holy **Trinity** is eternal, without beginning or end. At the creation of the world, God said, "Let *us* make man in *our* image" (Genesis
1:26). At Jesus' Baptism in the Jordan River, God the Holy Spirit
descended on Jesus as a dove, and God the Father's voice proclaimed
that Jesus is His Son. In the Church, Christians are baptized into the
name of the triune God—the Father, Son, and Holy Spirit.

Long ago, in the days after Jesus ascended into heaven, there were false teachers who did not believe in the triune God. The first Christians defended the teaching of the Trinity by composing three **creeds** or confessions of faith: the **Apostles' Creed**, the **Nicene Creed**, and the **Athanasian Creed**. Some of the earliest hymns sung in churches teach about the Trinity. The Church also developed a number of symbols for the Trinity, which helped to speak the truth. Each symbol tells the story of one God in three persons.

The first and most common symbol of the Holy Trinity combines three circles, one for each person of the Trinity: the Father, Son, and Holy Spirit. The circles are intertwined to show that these three persons are joined as one. A trefoil, a leaf with three circle parts like a clover, is similar in meaning.

An equilateral triangle is one of the oldest symbols for the Holy Trinity. Its sides and angles are of equal length, none of them greater than the other. Sometimes the three circles and the triangle are combined along with the symbols for each person of the Holy Trinity.

The creeds lead us in confessing that God is three persons in one. The creeds, sometimes called **symbols,** help us understand what cannot be seen. The symbols like the triangle and the interlocking circle help us visualize the Holy Trinity.

Lord God Almighty, unto Thee be glory,
    One in three persons, over all exalted!
Glory we offer, praise Thee and adore Thee,
    Now and forever. *LSB 504:4*

Symbols about God the Father

I believe in God, the Father Almighty, Maker of heaven and earth.
—*The Apostles' Creed, First Petition*

The most common symbol for God the Father is the **Manus Dei**, Latin words that mean, "the hand of God." This image illustrates God the Creator who is over and above all things. By His own hand He has "made me and all creatures; . . . He richly and daily provides me with all that I need to support this body and life" (Small Catechism, First Article). While there are several variations of this symbol, the Manus Dei is often shown as a hand opening downward out of a bright cloud.

Another form of the Manus Dei shows the hand with three fingers extended to represent the three persons of the Holy Trinity. The two closed fingers remind us of the two natures of Christ who is both God and man. Your pastor may hold his fingers in this way when he gives you the blessing of God.

In some Christian traditions, angels, apostles, martyrs, and other Christians of great distinction are identified by a circle behind them. This circle is called a **nimbus**. Surrounding the Manus Dei, there is likely to be a nimbus. This nimbus has a cross at its center. The nimbus with the cross is only used with the images and symbols that represent the triune God—God the Father, God the Son, or God the Holy Spirit.

8

Symbols of the Old Testament

Now the serpent was more crafty than any other beast of the field that the Lord God had made. He said to the woman, "Did God actually say, 'You shall not eat of any tree in the garden'?"

GENESIS 3:1

From the beginning, all three persons of the Holy Trinity have been active in the lives of God's people. In the Old Testament, the words and actions of God the Father are most prominent. The Old Testament is filled with the picture language of God, telling the story of His mercy and goodness toward sinful humanity. Once you learn to spot and read God's picture language, you will find there are many symbols in all of God's Word, but especially so in the Old Testament. The next few symbols are a place to start.

The serpent wrapped around the trunk of a fruit tree tells the story of man's fall into sin.

Satan disguised himself as a serpent and tempted Eve to eat the forbidden fruit of the tree of the knowledge of good and evil. Eve ate of the fruit and so did Adam. Because of their sin, God made Adam and Eve leave the garden and put an angel with a flaming sword at the entrance as a sign of His authority.

The symbol of a snake coiled around the globe reminds us of the sad truth that the sin of Adam and Eve brought sin and death to the whole world.

All mankind fell in Adam's fall;
     One common sin infects us all.
From one to all the curse descends,
     And over all God's wrath impends. *LSB 562:1*

And God said, "This is the sign of the covenant that I make between Me and you and every living creature that is with you, for all future generations: I have set My bow in the cloud, and it shall be a sign of the covenant between Me and the earth."

GENESIS 9:11–13

God created people with eyes to see and minds that could understand. God knew that His children would need visible **signs** to teach and assure them of His promises and loving presence. The story of Noah is one in which God provides a symbol that the people can see and so trust God's Word. The rainbow is the sign of the **covenant**, or symbol, of God's promise to Noah to never again flood the earth. Even now, when a rainbow appears or is pictured, it is a symbol of the truth of God's Word and the certainty of God's promise.

After the rain stopped, a dove was sent out and returned to the ark with a fresh olive leaf. This was the sign to Noah that the floodwaters were going down, and the earth was at peace. The picture of a dove with a leaf or branch in its mouth tells the story of the flood and of true peace, which only comes from God.

The image of the ark has become a symbol for the Church. Just as in the ark, God saved Noah and his family, keeping them safe from the flood. In the Church, God keeps you safe from sin, death, and the devil through His Word and **Sacraments**. The inside space of the church is called the **nave**, a word that means ship.

The Lord said to Moses, *"Come up to Me on the mountain and wait there, that I may give you the tables of stone, with the law and the commandment, which I have written for their instruction."*

EXODUS 24:12

Another Old Testament story that points us to Christ is the story of when God gave His Law, the Ten Commandments, to Moses. The Commandments were first written on two tablets of stone that Moses brought down from the mountain after a meeting with God. When we see the image of two stone tablets, we recognize it as the symbol for God's Law.

All people sin and do not keep God's commandments. In the time before Jesus, the people of God sacrificed offerings of grain and animals to pay for their sins. The sacrifices were burned on altars of stone. The symbol of a pile of stones with flames on top recalls these sacrifices for sin. God sent His Son, Jesus, to be the perfect and final sacrifice for you. His death on the cross was the sacrifice for all sin.

God's people also offer sacrifices of praise and thanks to God for His goodness and mercy toward them. These sacrifices are joined with songs of praise as we gather together to worship God. In the days of old, there were no organs or pianos to accompany singing. The Bible records various kinds of trumpets, drums, and stringed instruments. The harp, a stringed instrument, has become a symbol for the musical praise and worship of God.

Let my prayer rise before You as incense, the lifting up of my hands as the evening sacrifice.

—*Psalmody for Evening Prayer, LSB, p. 245*

Symbols of God the Son

[I believe] in Jesus Christ, His only Son, our Lord, who was conceived by the Holy Spirit, born of the Virgin Mary, suffered under Pontius Pilate, was crucified, died and was buried. He descended into hell. The third day He rose again from the dead. He ascended into heaven and sits at the right hand of God the Father Almighty. From thence He will come to judge the living and the dead.

—*The Apostles' Creed, Second Article*

Using God's Word as their guide, the first Christians developed many symbols for Jesus. They used symbols in underground caves and caverns to mark the graves of those who had died. Later, symbols were painted and carved on the walls and furnishings of churches. Today, these same symbols are recognized and repeated by God's people in homes and churches all over the world.

Jesus told His **disciples** that He was the true vine and that those who trust in Him for salvation are branches of the vine. In order to produce fruit and stay green, the branches need to be attached to the vine. We stay attached to Jesus through His Word and Sacraments. Church art uses the symbol of the vine to represent Jesus, the true vine, and our relationship with Him.

Worthy are You, to take the scroll and to open its seals,
for You were slain, and by Your blood You ransomed
people for God from every tribe and language and people
and nation, and You have made them a kingdom and priests
to our God, and they shall reign on the earth.

REVELATION 5:9–10

The **Agnus Dei**, the Lamb of God, is one of the most frequently used symbols for our Lord Jesus Christ. The lamb reminds us that payment for sin required a sacrifice, and that Jesus was the ultimate and final sacrifice for sin. Jesus is the Lamb of God foretold by Isaiah and John the Baptist. The Agnus Dei stands with a victor's flag and tells the story of Christ's victory over sin and death. The Agnus Dei is sometimes shown resting on a book with seven seals. This symbol comes from Revelation, where St. John tells us that the Lamb of God is the only one who can break these heavenly seals and open heaven to us.

At the Lamb's high feast we sing
    Praise to our victorious King,
Who has washed us in the tide
    Flowing from His side. *LSB* 633:1

And we have seen and testify that the Father has sent
His Son to be the Savior of the world. Whoever confesses that
Jesus is the Son of God, God abides in him, and he in God.

1 JOHN 4:14–15

In the early days of Christianity the people of God were persecuted for their faith in Jesus. The rulers of the Roman Empire made it illegal to believe or worship Jesus. If Christians were discovered, they might have been arrested, beaten, and imprisoned. Many were **martyred** for their faith in Jesus. The harsh rules against Christians forced God's people to create a secret code language in order to communicate with one another. One of these secret code-words is the Greek word *ICHTHUS* (ἰχθύς, capitalized ΙΧΘΥΣ) which means "fish."

The Greek letters that spelled fish—ICHTHUS—and the picture of a fish is one of the most popular symbols for Jesus! The Greek letters in the word ICHTHUS form an acronym for "Jesus Christ, Son of God, Savior." In this one little word for fish, a Christian could profess his faith in Jesus Christ as his Savior to another Christian!

Ιησους = Jesus (Matthew 1:20–21)

Χριστος = Christ (Matthew 16:13–20)

Θεος = God (John 1:1–4)

Υίος = Son (John 1:32–34)

Σωτηρ = Savior (Romans 10:9–10)

Jesus used many picture words to describe Himself. The Church has turned these into symbols that we use to learn and remember who Jesus is. Scripture tells us that Jesus called Himself many names, such as the Vine, the Way, the Door, the Gate, the Life, the Light of the World, the Bread of Life, the Bridegroom, the Chief Cornerstone, and the Good Shepherd. The apostles and disciples of Jesus also used picture language when speaking or writing about Jesus: the King of kings, the Word, the Righteous Branch, the Rock, the Morning Star, the Living Stone, Lion of the Tribe of Judah, and many others. Each name and symbol for Jesus reveals more about Him and who He is for us.

All who confess Christ's holy name,
　　Give God the praise and glory.
Let all who know His pow'r proclaim
　　Aloud the wondrous story.
　　Cast ev'ry idol from its throne,
For God is God, and He alone:
　　To God all praise and glory! *LSB* 819:5

I am the Alpha and Omega, the first and the last,
the beginning and the end.

REVELATION 22:13

The Alpha and the Omega are the symbols for the first and last letters of the Greek alphabet. These two Greek letters are frequently used to symbolize Jesus, the living Lord, who is both first and last, the beginning and the end.

In the Apostles' Creed we confess that Jesus ascended into heaven and sits at the right hand of God the Father Almighty, where He will judge the living and the dead. The symbol of Christ the Judge shows Jesus sitting on a throne, holding a cross and orb. On the Last Day, Jesus will come to judge the world, and He will take all who believe in Him for salvation to live with Him in heaven.

Two other Greek letters are used as a symbol for Jesus. The ancient Chi Rho symbol is an abbreviation for the Greek word for Christ. Another letter symbol you have likely seen is of the Greek word for Jesus. Both the Chi Rho and IHC or IHS are abbreviations for the names Christ and Jesus.

You sit at the right hand of God in the glory of the Father. We believe that You will come to be our judge.

—The Te Deum, LSB, p. 224

The Cross

For in Him all the fullness of God was pleased to dwell, and through Him to reconcile to Himself all things, whether on earth or in heaven, making peace by the blood of His cross.

COLOSSIANS 1:19–20

Of all the symbols that point people to Jesus, there is one that stands out from all the rest. The cross, in its many forms, is the universal symbol for Christ and His Church. On the cross, God's Son, Jesus Christ, suffered and died for you and all people, paying for the sins of the whole world. Because Jesus suffered and died and rose to life on **Easter** morning, when you die, you will rise to new life and live forever with Jesus in heaven. The **crucifix** is a cross with the figure of our crucified Lord upon it. This cross is a symbol of the suffering and death Jesus endured to atone for the sin of the world.

Cross of Jesus, cross of sorrow,
  Where the blood of Christ was shed,
Perfect man on thee did suffer,
  perfect God on thee has bled!
Here the King of all the ages,
  Throned in light ere worlds could be,
Robed in mortal flesh is dying,
  Crucified by sin for me. *LSB* 428:1–2

There are over 400 types of crosses, but the Christian Church uses only 50 or so of them. Look around your church and see how many different types of crosses you can find. The cross seen most often in every kind of Christian Church is the Latin cross. This simple cross looks like the small letter t.

The graded cross is the one that is often used on altars. The cross rests upon three steps or grades. These steps form the base of the cross so it can stand freely. The steps are said to represent faith, hope, and love, with faith being the top step.

A cross with four equal arms is known as the Greek cross. This cross is most often found on the altar where five Greek crosses are embroidered onto the white, **fair linen** cloth. The Greek crosses are found at each corner with one in the center, symbolizing the five wounds of Jesus. When the **Lord's Supper** is served from the altar, the vessels that contain the body and blood of Jesus rest over the center Greek cross. This group of five Greek crosses is sometimes also found carved into the stone or wood of the altar itself.

The Tau cross looks like the Greek letter Tau, or like the capital letter T. This cross symbolizes the Old Testament prophecies about Jesus. The Tau cross reminds us of the lifting up of the pole with the serpent by Moses when many snakes were biting the people of God. Those who looked at the pole that God provided were saved from the deadly snakes. God provided His Son, Jesus, who was raised up on a cross to save us from deadly sin. We look to Jesus for our salvation.

An anchor and a cross combined symbolizes the hope of salvation which is anchored in Christ's death and resurrection on the cross.

A cross on a shield is called the shield of faith. A shield is used by soldiers to protect them from being hurt by the enemy. A shield comes between the person and the danger. This symbol helps us to remember how Christ's death and resurrection protects from sin, coming between us and death and the devil.

The Holy Spirit

I believe in the Holy Spirit, the holy Christian church, the communion of saints, the forgiveness of sins, the resurrection of the body, and the life everlasting. Amen.

—The Apostles' Creed, Third Article

We have seen that there are many symbols that help us picture God the Father and God the Son. The symbols for the third person of the Holy Trinity, God the Holy Spirit, are few in number. The most common, and one of the oldest, symbol is a descending dove.

And when Jesus was baptized, immediately He went up from the water, and behold, the heavens were opened to Him, and He saw the Spirit of God descending like a dove and coming to rest on Him; and behold, a voice from heaven said, "This is My beloved Son, with whom I am well pleased."

MATTHEW 3:16–17

At **Pentecost**, the Holy Spirit appeared as a flame on the heads of the disciples filling them with His gifts (Acts 2:2–4). Suddenly, they could preach about salvation in Jesus Christ in many different languages, languages they had never spoken, so that all who were there could understand and believe.

The second most common symbol for God the Holy Spirit is a seven-tongued flame of fire. The seven tongues of the flame represent the seven gifts of the Holy Spirit: wisdom, understanding, counsel, strength, knowledge, fear of the Lord, and delight in the fear of the Lord. This symbol recalls what happened at Pentecost.

The dove and seven-tongued flame, symbols for the Holy Spirit, are found on the red banners, **vestments**, and altar **paraments** for the days of Pentecost, Baptism, Confirmation, and for an Ordination. These symbols proclaim that the power to believe, confess, and preach the Good News about Jesus Christ comes only through the Holy Spirit through the Word of God.

The Word of God

All Scripture is breathed out by God.

2 TIMOTHY 3:16

The Holy Spirit comes to us in and through God's Word. He gives us faith in Jesus, and through the Word, strengthens and keeps us in the faith. In the church, an open book, laying flat, is a familiar symbol for God's Word. Maybe you have seen a more ancient symbol—that of two scrolls, one each for the Old and New Testaments. Another symbol for God's Word is that of an oil lamp lit with flame. The psalmist tells us: "Your word is a lamp to my feet and a light to my path" (Psalm 119:105).

As I pray, dear Jesus, hear me;
    Let Your words in me take root.
May Your Spirit e'er be near me
    That I bear abundant fruit. *LSB 589:4*

The Sacrament of Holy Baptism

But with the Word of God it is a Baptism, that is, a life-giving water, rich in grace, and a washing of the new birth in the Holy Spirit.

—Small Catechism, Baptism, Third Part

The Holy Spirit joins God's Word and simple water in the Sacrament of **Holy Baptism** and grants forgiveness, life, and salvation to all who believe. The pastor baptizes in the name of the triune God, the Father, Son, and Holy Spirit.

The **font** is the universal symbol of Holy Baptism, reminding all who see it that through Word and water sins are washed away and a child of God is born. In Holy Baptism, it is customary to use a shell as a scoop for the water. The symbol of the shell with three drops of water beneath it proclaims that Baptism is in the name of the Father and the Son and Holy Spirit.

The Office of the Keys

Two keys crossed form the symbol for the **Office of the Keys**. The one key represents forgiveness of sin, which unlocks and opens the door to eternal life for the repentant sinner. The other key represents a locked door keeping the one who does not repent of his sins from the blessings of forgiveness, life, and salvation.

My loving Father, here You take me
    To be henceforth Your child and heir.
My faithful Savior, here You make me
    The fruit of all Your sorrows share.
O Holy Spirit, comfort me
    When threat'ning clouds around I see. *LSB 590:2*

The Sacrament of the Altar

Our Lord Jesus Christ, on the night when He was betrayed, took bread, and when He had given thanks, He broke it and gave it to the disciples and said: "Take, eat; this is My body, which is given for you. This do in remembrance of Me."

In the same way also He took the cup after supper, and when He had given thanks, He gave it to them, saying: "Drink of it all of you; this cup is the new testament in My blood, which is shed for you for the forgiveness of sins. This do, as often as you drink it, in remembrance of Me." —*LSB, p. 162*

When the Holy Spirit joins God's Word with bread and wine in the **Sacrament of the Altar**, the people of God receive the body and blood of Jesus given and shed for them. In this holy meal, God grants forgiveness of sins, rescue from death and the devil, and eternal life to all who believe.

Following the **Words of our Lord** in the Divine Service, the pastor holds up the **chalice** and **host** and says to the people: "The peace of the Lord be with you always." The image of a chalice and the host together is the perfect and most common symbol for the Lord's Supper. Another symbol used is that of grapes and wheat. Together these symbolize the physical elements that combine with the Word of God in this holy meal.

Look for the two **Eucharist** lights in your church. When these two candles on the altar are lit, they proclaim that the Lord's Supper will be celebrated in the service. The candlelight testifies to the presence of Jesus, the light of the world, who comes to us through the Word and Holy Communion.

An ancient symbol for the Lord's Supper tells a beautiful legend of a mother pelican in the nest with her hungry little ones. Because they will die without food to keep them alive, she allows them to drink her blood so that they will live. In doing so, the mother will die. In fact, mother pelicans do not feed their children in this way. But our Lord does feed us with His own flesh and blood that He shed on the cross, which nourishes and strengthens us for this life and gives us life eternal. This symbol is known as the Pelican-in-Her-Piety.

Thou, like the pelican to feed her brood,
    Didst pierce Thyself to give us living food;
Thy blood, O Lord, one drop has power to win
    Forgiveness for our world and all its sin. *LSB* 640:3

Prayers

With these words God tenderly invites us to believe that He is our true father and that we are His true children, so that with all boldness and confidence we may ask Him as dear children ask their dear father.
—*Small Catechism, The Lord's Prayer, Introduction*

From the beginning of time God's people have offered praise, thanksgiving, and requests to God in prayer. God in His Word tells us to pray always. God provides the Book of Psalms, the prayer book of the Bible, filled with 150 prayers that God's people have prayed repeatedly since ancient days.

In the Old Testament, prayer was an important part of the worship service. Prayers to God were accompanied by the burning of sweet smelling incense. The smoke of the incense burning inside a container would drift upward as the prayers of the people rose up to heaven. From the earliest days the symbol for prayer has been a censor with the rising smoke coming out of it. In the liturgy of Evening Prayer, we sing, "Let my prayer rise before You as incense," a passage which comes from Psalm 141:2.

Jesus' disciples asked Him to teach them how to pray. He answered: "When you pray, say: 'Father, hallowed be Your name' " (Luke 11:2). What He taught them was the Lord's Prayer. Martin

Luther said, "There is no nobler prayer to be found upon earth than the Lords' Prayer" (Large Catechism, Part 3, paragraph 23).

In our day, the image of folded hands or a person kneeling with folded hands is a familiar symbol for prayer. Kneeling, closing your eyes, bowing your head, and folding your hands or arms are all good positions for prayer because they help to still your body and focus your thoughts on speaking to God.

Let my prayer rise before You as incense, and the lifting up of my hands as the evening sacrifice. —*LSB, p. 231*

Advent

And behold, you will conceive in your womb and bear a son, and you shall call His name Jesus. He will be great and will be called the Son of the Most High. And the Lord God will give to Him the throne of His father David, and He will reign over the house of Jacob forever, and of His kingdom there will be no end.

LUKE 1:31–33

The Church's calendar marks special seasons and days that follow the life of Christ and the Church. The **Church Year** begins with the first Sunday of the season of **Advent**.

Advent is a time of repentance and preparation as God's people await the coming of their Savior and King. The symbols of Advent flow out of the Old Testament prophecies about the coming Messiah. These prophecies point to the Son of God, who entered this world as a human baby, who suffered and died, and who rose again for you. Jesus now prepares a place for you in heaven and will on the last day return to take all believers there for eternity.

The ancient Advent hymn "O Come, O Come, Emmanuel" recalls seven prophecies about Jesus. The symbols for these seven prophecies are:

O Wisdom Jesus is the wisdom of God who lights the path of knowledge and teaches us in the way we should go.

O Adonai *Adonai* means "Lord." Jesus is the Lord of might and king of all creation. He comes with outstretched arms to redeem us.

O Root of Jesse New life shoots from the dead stump. Jesus is the promised Messiah who comes to redeem us from the tyranny of Satan. By His death we have life forever.

O Key of David Jesus is the key that opens heaven to all who trust in Him for their salvation.

O Dayspring Jesus is the dayspring who brings eternal light and life, chasing away the darkness of sin and death forever.

O Desire of Nations Jesus is the desire of not only Israel, but of all the nations who have waited and watched for the true Savior to come.

O Emmanuel Jesus is God's Son made man and born to the Virgin Mary. *Emmanuel* means "God with us." Jesus lived among us on earth and remains God with us in His Word and in the sacraments of Holy Baptism and The Lord's Supper.

O come, O come, Emmanuel,
    And ransom captive Israel,
That mourns in lonely exile here
    Until the Son of God appear.
Rejoice! Rejoice! Emmanuel
    Shall come to thee, O Israel! *LSB* 357:1

Christmas

When the angels went away from them into heaven,
the shepherds said to one another, "Let us go over to Bethlehem
and see this thing that has happened, which the Lord has
made known to us." And they went with haste and found
Mary and Joseph and the baby lying in a manger.

LUKE 2:15–16

The symbols for **Christmas** helps us remember that God became man in the person of Jesus Christ in order to save the world from sin and death.

The most common Christmas symbol is a manger. Sometimes the manger is shown with the baby Jesus and sometimes with a star shining above the manger, recalling the star that God placed in the sky over Bethlehem when Jesus was born. Another symbol for Christmas is a shepherd's crook, which reminds us of the shepherds in the field who after hearing about Jesus from the angels came to worship Him in the manger. Sometimes the image of a rose is used to depict the Nativity of our Lord. This symbol is called the Christmas Rose.

Epiphany

Epiphany is both a special day and a season in the Church Year. During Epiphany, the Church recalls the Wise Men from the East who came with gifts to see the baby Jesus. The Wise Men followed the star that God placed in the sky over Bethlehem. The symbol seen most often to mark Epiphany is a shining star. The shining star reflects the truth that Jesus Christ is the light of the world who shines the light of life and chases away the darkness of sin and death. The symbol of three travelers upon camels is also used to indicate Epiphany, as is the image of three gifts.

Lord, now You let Your servant go in peace; Your word has been fulfilled. My own eyes have seen the salvation which You have prepared in the sight of every people: A light to reveal You to the nations and the glory of Your people Israel.

—Nunc Dimittis, LSB, p.165

Symbols of our Lord's Passion

And when they came to the place that is called The Skull,
there they crucified Him, and the criminals, one on His right
and one on His left. And Jesus said, "Father, forgive them,
for they know not what they do."

LUKE 23:33–34

Lent is the season following Epiphany in the Church Year. It begins a journey for God's people recalling the events leading up to the **Passion of our Lord** as He suffered and died for the sins of the world. Lent is a season of repentance and prayer.

Nearly all the symbols used in Lent flow from the events which began on Palm Sunday, culminating in Christ's death upon the cross and His resurrection on Easter morning.

We have already looked at the cross and some of its many variations. God loved you so much that He gave His only Son to suffer and die for you. The crucifix is a perfectly wonderful symbol of God's love.

Palm fronds crossed alone or over a crown symbolize the royal entrance of Jesus into Jerusalem on Palm Sunday. A lantern or torch reminds us of the betrayal in the Garden of Gethsemane, as does a drawstring pouch with coins. A circle of thorns reminds us of the prickly crown that was put on Jesus' head as the people mocked Him, calling Him "King of the Jews." A seamless tunic with three dice or a pair of dice recalls when the soldiers rolled the dice to decide who would receive the divided the garments of Jesus. A rooster is the symbol of Peter's denial of Jesus. The image of three nails tells the story of how our Lord's hands and feet were nailed to the cross. You may see some or all of these symbols combined together on a banner, bulletin, or paraments and vestments at your church.

Lamb of God, You take away the sin of the world; have mercy on us.
Lamb of God, You take away the sin of the world; have mercy on us.
Lamb of God, You take away the sin of the world; grant us peace.

—*Agnus Dei, LSB, p.163*

Easter

But on the first day of the week, at early dawn,
they went to the tomb, taking the spices they had prepared.
And they found the stone rolled away from the tomb.

LUKE 24:1–2

Easter and its joyous season follow the somber time of Lent. The transition between Lent and Easter in the Church is dramatic. The sights, sounds, and smells of Easter proclaim the glorious news of the Resurrection of our Lord.

The sound of trumpets, the white Easter lily with it sweet smell, the empty cross with the white cloth draped upon it, are all familiar sights. There are some less-familiar symbols for Easter, and each of these tells us something about what this holy day means for us.

A butterfly is a symbol of the resurrection because the caterpillar must first wrap itself in a tomblike chrysalis and die before it can turn into a beautiful butterfly. Jesus died on the cross, was wrapped in cloths, and was laid in a tomb. Three days later Jesus was raised from the dead.

One popular symbol of resurrection is based on the legend of the Phoenix. After living for about 500 years, the Phoenix would then built a nest and was set aflame, completely burned up in the fire. Out of the ashes left from the fire, a young living bird arises and flies away. Though the Phoenix is just a story, Jesus' death and resurrection are very true. Because of Jesus' death and resurrection, when you die, you will rise again to live forever.

A crown seen on Easter proclaims that Jesus is truly the King of kings. As His child, you will one day receive the crown of life eternal.

A bursting pomegranate is another symbol often used of Jesus bursting forth from tomb on Easter morn. The many seeds inside this fruit that burst out when it is ripe also represent all believers in Jesus who will one day burst from their tombs.

The Agnus Dei, the Lamb of God, is a symbol with much meaning, as explained on page 15. You will see the Agnus Dei on Easter because in this symbol the Lamb of God holds a white flag with a red cross. This is the flag of victory—victory over the grave, won by the lamb, your Savior Jesus.

Evangelists and Apostles

Go therefore and make disciples of all nations, baptizing them in the name of the Father and of the Son and of the Holy Spirit, teaching them to observe all that I have commanded you. And behold, I am with you always, to the end of the age.

MATTHEW 28:18–20

When Jesus walked upon this earth, He gathered to Himself a group of men. The men left their work and their homes to follow Jesus. These companions of Jesus became His disciples. God used these men in special ways, working through them to establish the Christian Church and to preach and record God's Word.

The first of these men are the four **evangelists**—Matthew, Mark, Luke, and John. Their symbols date to the early days of the Christian Church. An evangelist is one who proclaims the Word of God. Their symbols help us to understand what these men thought important to

write down about Jesus. Their writings are the first four books of the New Testament, known as the **Gospels**. In each of the four Gospel writers' symbols, the wings and the nimbus tell us that Jesus was true God.

The symbol of St. Matthew is the winged man that looks much like an angel. In His Gospel, Matthew wrote about Jesus' human family and His incarnation, the fact that Jesus is both true God and true man.

St. Mark's symbol is a winged lion because the beginning of Mark's Gospel is about John the Baptist, the voice of one crying in the wilderness. His preaching about Jesus was bold like a roaring lion.

A winged ox is the symbol for St. Luke. This symbol reminds us that Luke gave the fullest account of Jesus' suffering and death as the sacrifice for sin. An ox is an animal of sacrifice. Jesus is the final and complete sacrifice.

St. John's symbol is an eagle flying upward to the sky. The Gospel of St. John is written in such a way that its words seem to soar as if on eagles wings and thus reminds us of Christ's ascension to heaven after Easter.

Saints, see the cloud of witnesses surround us;
    Their lives of faith encourage and astound us.
Hear how the Master praised their faith so fervent:
    "Well done, My servant!" *LSB 667:1*

Apostles

In these days He went out to the mountain to pray,
and all night He continued in prayer to God.
And when day came, He called His disciples and chose
from them twelve, whom He named apostles.

LUKE 6:12

The **apostles** were the disciples of Jesus sent out to preach and teach to all the world. These were the men present in the Upper Room when Jesus appeared to them after rising from the dead. They were the same men gathered together on Pentecost when the gifts of the Holy Spirit and fire were given. Sometimes, St. John the Baptist is included as an apostle, as well as St. Paul, who was made an apostle after Pentecost.

Each apostle has several different symbols. These symbols point to something known about the apostle's life or how the apostle died in the faith.

St. Peter is the apostle who made the great confession when Jesus asked, "Who do you say that I am?" Peter's answer was certain and sure: "You are the Christ, the Son of the living God" (Matthew 16:15–16). Jesus said He would build His Church on the foundation of Peter's confession and give to the Church the keys to the kingdom of heaven. Peter's symbol shows two keys, and sometimes they are placed over an upside down cross, the way in which Peter died.

St. James the Greater was one of the disciples closest to Jesus. Herod beheaded him for making a bold confession of faith. His confession caused others to boldly confess Jesus as their Savior and Lord. St. James was known as a pilgrim—his home was heaven. His symbol indicates his pilgrim or traveling life, with the image of three escalloped shells.

St. John the Evangelist has a different symbol when he is included with the apostles. His apostolic symbol is a chalice with a serpent inside it. This image recalls when he was given a chalice filled with poison. The Lord spared him, and he lived. He was beloved by Jesus.

St. Andrew's symbol is very simple. It shows the way he died. He was put on a saltire (X-shaped) cross for his faith in Jesus. While he was nailed to the cross, St. Andrew continued to confess and preach about Jesus.

These saints of old received God's commendation;
    They lived as pilgrim-heirs of His salvation.
Through faith they conquered flame and sword and gallows,
    God's name to hallow. *LSB 667:2*

And He called to Him His twelve disciples and gave them authority over unclean spirits, to cast them out, and to heal every disease and every affliction.

MATTHEW 10:1

St. Philip is remembered for his part in the feeding of the five thousand. One of his symbols recalls when he brought the two loaves of bread to Jesus. The long slender cross between the loaves reminds us that he proclaimed Christ crucified and risen. He died a martyr by cross and spear.

St. Bartholomew is sometimes known as Nathanael. His symbol shows that he died for his faith in Jesus. The knife was used to cut him open, and then he was put on a cross. The book represents God's Word, which he believed and preached to the very end of his life.

St. Thomas traveled to India to preach the Gospel. The carpenter's square reminds that while he was there he built a church with his own hands. The spear is the sign of how he died in India.

St. James the Less was a faithful follower and preacher of Jesus. His symbol tells us of his death when he was ninety-six years old. After dying a brutal martyr's death, his body was sawed into pieces.

St. Matthew left his position as a tax collector to follow Jesus. Three moneybags are the symbol for St. Matthew the apostle who died on a Tau cross in Ethiopia.

St. Jude is also known as Thaddaeus. His symbol tells the story of his travels with St. Simon on their missionary journeys. It is a sailing ship with a cross-shaped mast. St. Jude traveled to many places to preach the good news about Jesus.

St. Simon, the traveling partner for St. Jude, is most often shown with a symbol of a fish upon a book. Simon was a great fisher of men by the power of Gospel.

Judas Iscariot is the apostle who betrayed Jesus to the soldiers in the garden for 30 pieces of silver. His shield is most often shown blank with nothing on it. It reminds us how serious it is to deny our Lord.

St. Matthias had been with Jesus from the start. His election as the one to replace Judas, was done by casting lots. His symbol is a book showing his life's work to spread the Gospel with the axe that tells us his work led to his death for being a Christian.

St. Paul once was a fierce persecutor of Christians. Then God made him a bold preacher for Christ. His symbol is an open Bible, a sword, and the Latin words *Spiritus Gladius*, sword of the Spirit, which tells us that the sword of the Spirit is the Word of God.

You, Jesus, You alone deserve all glory!
  Our lives unfold, embraced within Your story;
Past, present, future—You the same forever—

Luther's Rose

In Luther's day it was a common practice for prominent members of the community to have a personal seal. The symbolism on the seal would tell others something about the person, what they did or believed. Through his bold preaching and teaching about the Word of God, Martin Luther had become well known. So it was that he was invited to create a personal seal in the year 1520. The most important thing to Martin Luther was his faith in Jesus Christ as his Savior from sin, death, and the devil. Luther's seal is rich with symbols and color. Each color has an important meaning.

Luther's seal clearly speaks what He believed about his salvation. He wrote it down, calling it the "summary of my [theology], belief in God."

The Meaning of Luther's Seal

The black cross in the center of a red heart reminds us that faith in Jesus who died on the cross is what saves us. The red heart is a message that one who believes this in his own heart will be saved. The black of the cross does not change the living, natural red color of the heart. This is so because the cross does not kill; it keeps us alive. Such a heart should stand inside a white rose to show that faith gives joy, comfort, and peace—gifts which come from the Holy Spirit. White is the color of the spirit and the angels. The rose should be surrounded by a sky-blue background, symbolizing that this joy and faith are the beginning of the heavenly joy and new life God gives to all who believe and trust in Him. Finally, the golden ring surrounding the seal reminds us that this heavenly, joyous life lasts forever without end. Just as gold is the best and most valuable metal, so the blessedness of heaven is beyond all joy and good things.

Glossary

Adonai. Hebrew for "Lord"; a name for Jesus.

Advent. From Latin *advenire,* meaning "to come unto." The season of preparation marked by the four Sundays before Christmas. During this time the Church looks forward to Jesus coming into the world.

Agnus Dei. Latin for "Lamb of God"; designation given to Jesus by John the Baptist (John 1:29).

altar. A stone or wooden structure at the center of the chancel. Church altars provide focus of the congregation's worship and the sacramental focus as the place from which God gives His gifts.

apostle. One sent directly by Christ into the world to carry out the Great Commission (Matthew 28:16–20).

Apostles' Creed. *See* Creed.

Athanasian Creed. *See* Creed.

Baptism, Holy. Sacrament by which the Holy Spirit creates faith through the application of water connected with God's Word.

chalice. From the Latin for "cup"; traditionally a gold or silver cup lined with gold; used to distribute wine at Holy Communion; may be made of ceramic, glass, or even wood.

Christmas. The time of the Church Year that focuses on the Father sending the Son to save the world; includes the seasons of Advent, Christmas, and Epiphany.

Church Year. The Church's calendar organized to observe the events in the life of Christ and the Church.

Communion, Holy. *See* Sacrament of the Altar.

covenant. From the Hebrew word for "to fetter," meaning "to bind or restrain." A covenant is a binding agreement between two parties or a promise made by one party to another.

creed. From the Latin word *credo,* "I believe"; a summary of what the Church believes; refers to any of the three Ecumenical Creeds used in worship: the Apostles' Creed, used at Baptisms, funerals, and non-Communion services; the Nicene Creed, often used at services with Holy Communion; the Athanasian Creed, often spoken on Trinity Sunday.

crucifix. A cross with the figure of the crucified Christ upon it.

disciple. A student or follower; one who follows Christ Jesus and His teachings.

Easter. The celebration of the Resurrection of Our Lord, the day when Jesus rose from the tomb. The date of Easter is determined by the date of the first Sunday after the first full moon after the spring equinox.

Emmanuel. Hebrew for "God with us"; a name for Jesus.

Epiphany. The day celebrating Jesus' "revealing" as God in the flesh to the Gentile Magi; the eighth day after Christmas, January 6.

Eucharist. *See* Sacrament of the Altar.

evangelist. From the Greek words for "Gospel" and "messenger." One whom the Church has sent to preach the Gospel. Matthew, Mark, Luke, and John are the four evangelists in Scripture.

fair linen. Long, fine linen cloth placed over the altar and draping nearly to the floor; usually has five crosses representing the wounds of Jesus, symbolic of Christ's burial cloth.

font. Large basin or pool that holds water for Baptism.

Gospel. The Good News of God's gracious love in Christ for the redemption of the world; the first four books of the New Testament.

host. Latin for "sacrifice or victim"; individual Communion wafers; Christ Himself, who serves His gathered guests.

ICHTHUS. The Greek word for "fish", ICHTHUS is an acronym from the first letters of the Greek words "Jesus Christ, God's Son, Savior."

Lent. From the Latin for "spring"; a season of forty weekdays before Easter; a time of preparation and repentance before the celebration of the Resurrection of Our Lord.

Lord's Supper. *See* Sacrament of the Altar.

Manus Dei. Latin for "the hand of God."

martyr. From the Greek word for "witness"; someone who voluntarily suffers the penalty of death for witnessing about the Savior.

nave. Latin for "ship"; the main portion of a church building where people gather to worship and pray.

Nicene Creed. *See* creed.

nimbus. Latin for "cloud"; the round shape with a cross in it that often accompanies pictures or symbols of God the Father, Son, or Holy Spirit.

Office of the Keys. The authority given to the Church by God to forgive the sins of repentant sinners and to bind the sins to unrepentant sinners.

paraments. The colored cloths that are used to decorate the altar, pulpit, and lectern according to the seasons of the Church Year.

Glossary

Passion of our Lord. The time of Jesus' suffering and death as recorded in the Gospels.

Pentecost. From the Greek meaning "fifty." The day when the Holy Spirit gave the apostles the ability to preach the Gospel in many different languages, celebrated on the fiftieth day of Easter.

Sacrament of the Altar. The celebration of Christ's true body and blood in, with, and under the bread and wine; Christians eat and drink this sacrament for the forgiveness of sin; also called the Eucharist, the Lord's Supper, and Holy Communion.

Sacrament. From the Greek word "mystery"; a sacred act instituted by God in which God Himself has joined His Word of promise to a visible element and by which He offers, gives, and seals the forgiveness of sins earned by Christ.

sacrifice. To give up or destroy something, often in exchange for something else (verb); something offered to God (noun).

sign/symbol. A visual image that points to or represents something else, a greater reality.

Trinity, triune. One true God in three persons: Father, Son, and Holy Spirit.

vestments. The special clothing that the pastor wears during the Divine Service. The various vestments have symbolic meanings that teach us about the pastoral office. For example, the alb is the white robe the pastor wears at the Divine Service: it symbolizes the white robe of Christ's righteousness, which covers ours sins and thus "covers up" the individual person of the pastor who stands in the stead of Christ when he preaches God's Word, forgives sins, and conducts the Sacraments.

Words of our Lord. The words spoken by Christ when He instituted the Sacrament of the Altar (Matthew 26:26–28; Mark 14:22–24; Luke 22:19–20; 1 Corinthians 11:23–25); the pastor speaks these very words of Christ in the Service of the Sacrament at the consecration of the bread and wine.